Infocracy

Byung-Chul Han

Infocracy
Digitalization and the Crisis of Democracy

Translated by Daniel Steuer

polity

Originally published in German as *Infokratie. Digitalisierung und die Krise der Demokratie* © MSB Matthes & Seitz Berlin Verlagsgesellschaft mbH, Berlin 2021. All rights reserved.

This English edition © Polity Press, 2022.

3

Polity Press
65 Bridge Street
Cambridge CB2 1UR, UK

Polity Press
101 Station Landing
Suite 300
Medford, MA 02155, USA

ISBN-13: 978-1-5095-5297-9
ISBN-13: 978-1-5095-5298-6 (paperback)

A catalogue record for this book is available from the British Library.

Library of Congress Control Number: 2022932415

Typeset in 11.5 on 15pt Janson Text
by Cheshire Typesetting Ltd, Cuddington, Cheshire
Printed and bound in Great Britain by TJ Books Ltd, Padstow, Cornwall

The publisher has used its best endeavours to ensure that the URLs for external websites referred to in this book are correct and active at the time of going to press. However, the publisher has no responsibility for the websites and can make no guarantee that a site will remain live or that the content is or will remain appropriate.

Every effort has been made to trace all copyright holders, but if any have been overlooked the publisher will be pleased to include any necessary credits in any subsequent reprint or edition.

For further information on Polity, visit our website:
politybooks.com

CONTENTS

The Information Regime

With the term 'information regime' I refer to a form of domination in which information and its processing by algorithms and artificial intelligence have a decisive influence on social, economic and political processes. Under such a regime, what is exploited is *information* and *data* rather than *bodies* and *energies*, as is the case under disciplinary regimes. Power depends not on the possession of the means of production but on access to information that is used for psychopolitical surveillance and the control and prediction of behaviour. Information regimes are tied to information capitalism, which develops into surveillance capitalism and reduces human beings to *consumer cattle that provide data*.

The disciplinary regime is the form of domination characteristic of industrial capitalism. Its form is mechanical: each person is a cog in the disciplinary machinery of power. Disciplinary power enters the nerves and sinews, and 'out of a formless clay, an inapt Body', it produces a 'machine'.[1] It fabricates 'docile' bodies: 'A body is docile that may be subjected, used, transformed and improved.'[2] Docile bodies are production machines. They are not *bearers of data and information*; they are *bearers of energy*. Under a disciplinary regime, human beings are drilled to become *labouring cattle*.

Information capitalism uses communication and interconnectedness, rendering obsolete the disciplinary techniques of spatial isolation, the strict regulation of work, and physical training. The ideal of the information regime is not 'docility', with the compliance and obedience it implies. The submissive subject of the information regime is neither docile nor obedient. The information regime assumes rather that its subject is *free*, *authentic* and *creative*. This subject *produces itself* and *performs* itself.

Foucault's disciplinary regime uses isolation as a means of domination: 'isolation is the primary condition of total submission'.[3] The panopticon, with its isolated cells, is the ideal symbol of the disciplinary regime. Isolation, however, cannot be transferred on to the information regime, which exploits communication in particular. Under the information regime, surveillance takes place via data. The isolated inmates of the disciplinary panopticon do not produce data because they do *not communicate*.

The target of biopolitical disciplinary power is the body: 'For capitalist society, it was biopolitics, the biological, the somatic, the corporeal, that mattered more than anything else.'[4] The biopolitical regime inserts the body into a production and surveillance machinery that optimizes it by way of a disciplinary orthopaedics. The information regime, whose emergence Foucault appears to have missed, does not pursue a *biopolitical agenda*. It is not interested in the body. It seizes *the psyche* by way of a *psychopolitics*. The body is now mainly understood in terms of aesthetics and fitness. At least in Western information capitalism, the body has for the most part been liberated from the disciplinary power that drilled it to become a labouring machine. The body has instead been seized by the beauty industry.

Every form of rule pursues a specific *politics of visibility*. For a sovereign regime, ostentatious demonstrations of power are essential. The spectacle is its medium. The ruling power presents itself with theatrical glamour. Such *glamour* even legitimizes it. Ceremonies and symbols of power stabilize rule. Pageantry, symbols of violence, grim feasts and ceremonial punishments are all part of the theatre and spectacle staged by the ruling power. Physical torture is publicly exhibited to achieve the greatest effect. The hangman and the condemned are actors, and the public space is a stage. The power of sovereignty works through theatrical visibility. It is a power that exhibits and makes itself known, that boasts and shines. For it to flourish, those subjected to this power have mostly to remain invisible.

The pre-modern sovereign regime is a society of the spectacle, but the modern disciplinary regime is a society of surveillance. The glamorous celebration of sovereignty and spectacular demonstrations of power give way to unspectacular bureaucratic surveillance. People are placed 'neither in the amphitheatre, nor on the stage, but in the panoptic machine'.[5] The arrangement of visibility is turned around: it is not the rulers but those they dominate who are made visible. Disciplinary power makes itself invisible while imposing permanent visibility on its subjects. In order to give those in power constant access, the subjugated are constantly placed in the spotlight. 'The fact of constantly being seen . . . maintains the disciplined individual in his subjection.'[6]

The efficiency of the disciplinary panopticon consists in the fact that its inmates feel constantly observed. They internalize their surveillance. The creation of 'a state of conscious and permanent visibility' is essential to disciplinary power.[7] In George Orwell's surveillance state, it is Big Brother who ensures permanent visibility: *Big Brother is watching you*. Under the disciplinary regime, spatial measures such as confinement and isolation guarantee the visibility of the subjugated. The subjugated are assigned specific locations in space that they are not permitted to leave. Their mobility is severely limited so that they cannot avoid the panopticon.

In the information society, the disciplinary regime's structures of confinement dissolve into open networks. The information regime adheres to the following topological principles: discontinuities are reduced in favour of continuities; confinement gives way to openings; isolated cells are replaced with communicative networks. Visibility is now produced in a totally different way: *not through isolation but through interconnection*. Digital information technology turns communication into surveillance. The more data we generate and the more intensely we communicate, the more efficient surveillance becomes. The mobile phone is a surveillance and subjugation apparatus that exploits freedom and communication. Under the information regime, people do not feel that they are

4

under surveillance. They feel free. Paradoxically, it is the feeling of freedom that secures the rule of the regime. This is the fundamental difference between the information and the disciplinary regimes. *When freedom and surveillance coincide, domination becomes complete.*

The information regime has no need for disciplinary pressure. It does not impose panoptic visibility on people. People expose themselves out of an inner need – without any external compulsion. People *produce themselves*, that is, play to the gallery. The French verb *se produire* means *to present oneself*. Where the disciplinary regime imposes visibility, the information regime relies on the fact that people seek to be visible. They voluntarily enter the lime-light. Whereas the inmates of the disciplinary panopticon try to avoid visibility, the subjects of the information regime actually desire it.

The information regime pursues its policies in the name of *transparency*. To think of transparency exclusively in terms of institutions and individuals making information publicly available is to miss its true significance. Transparency is the *systemic compulsion of the information regime*. The imperative of transparency is: *everything has to be available as information.* Transparency and information are synonyms. The information society is a transparency society. The imperative of transparency is that information must circulate freely. It is not people but information that is truly free. The paradox of the information society is that *people are imprisoned by information*. By communicating and producing information, they shackle themselves. *The digital prison is transparent.*

Apple's flagship store in New York is a cube made of glass. It is a *temple to transparency*. With regard to visibility, it is the architectural counter-image of the Kaaba in Mecca. Kaaba literally means 'cube'. The Kaaba is invisible behind a thick black curtain. Only priests have access to the inside of the building. The *arcanum*, which rejects all visibility, is constitutive of the theo-political form of domination. The innermost space in a Greek temple, which is protected against visibility, is called *adyton* (literally: the inaccessible). Only priests may enter the sacred space. This form of domination is based on the *arcanum*. The transparent Apple store, by contrast, is open around the clock. The shop is located in the basement. Everyone – every customer – has access to the building. The Kaaba, with its black curtain, and the glass Apple store represent two different forms of rule: *arcanum and transparency*.

Although Apple's cube suggests freedom and unhindered communication, it is actually an embodiment of the *merciless rule of information*. The information regime renders people totally transparent, but domination itself is never transparent. *There is no transparent form of domination*. Transparency is merely the front of a process that is itself invisible. Transparency itself is not transparent. There is a reverse side to it. *The engine room of transparency lies in the dark*. We surrender to the growing power of the algorithmic black box.

The rule of the information regime is hidden because it is fully incorporated into everyday life. It hides behind the friendliness of social media, the convenience of search engines, the soothing voices of the virtual assistants and the courteous servility of smart apps. The smartphone is in fact an efficient *informant* that exposes us to 24/7 surveillance. The *smart home* turns a whole apartment into a digital prison in which our daily lives are recorded minute by minute. The smart vacuum cleaner may save us from some tedious cleaning, but it also maps our home. The *smart bed* and its networked sensors continue the surveillance while we sleep. Surveillance creeps into daily life by way of *convenience*. In the digital prison, this smart comfort zone, there is no resistance to the ruling regime. The *like* prevents any thought of revolution.

Information capitalism appropriates neoliberal technologies of power. Where the power technologies of the disciplinary regime worked with compulsion and prohibition, the neoliberal ones work with *positive incentives*. They exploit freedom instead of repressing it. They control our will at an unconscious level instead of violently breaking it. Repressive disciplinary power gives way to smart power, a power that does not give orders but *whispers*, that does not command but *nudges*. In other words, it *pokes* us with subtle tools that influence our behaviour. The *surveillance and punishment* of Foucault's disciplinary regime give way to *motivation and optimization*. Under the neoliberal information regime, domination presents itself as *freedom, communication and community*.

The influencers on YouTube and Instagram have internalized the neoliberal technologies of power. Whether they peddle travel, beauty or fitness, they constantly invoke freedom, creativity and authenticity. Their advertisements are not seen as annoying because the products are cleverly embedded in the influencers' self-presentation. Whereas people use ad-blockers to remove conventional advertisements on YouTube, they intentionally seek out the influencers' ads. Influencers are worshipped as idols, and this gives their presentations a religious character. Influencers claiming to be motivational coaches present themselves as saviours, and their followers, their disciples, take part in the influencers' lives by buying the products the influencers pretend to consume in staged scenes from their everyday life – a kind of *digital Eucharist*. Social media is a church: *like is 'amen'*; *sharing is communion*; *consumption is salvation*. The repetition that influencers use as a dramatic tool does not bore; rather, it gives the whole affair the *character of a liturgy*. At the same time, influencers present consumer products as means of self-realization. We consume ourselves to death while realizing ourselves to death. Consumption and identity become one. Identity itself becomes a commodity.

We imagine that we are free, but in reality our entire lives are recorded so that our behaviour might be psychopolitically controlled. Under the neoliberal information regime, mechanisms of power function not because people are aware of the fact of constant surveillance but because they *perceive* themselves to be *free*. Whereas Big Brother's telescreen is *untouchable*, the smart touchscreen makes everything available and consumable. It thereby produces the illusion of a 'freedom we have at our fingertips'.[8] Under the information regime, *being free* does not mean being able to act but being able to click, like and post. For this reason, there is little resistance to the regime. It need not fear revolution. Fingers, by themselves, are not capable of genuine action. They are only an *organ for making consumer choices*. Consumption and revolution exclude each other.

An important characteristic of classic totalitarianism, as a secular political religion, is that it makes a 'claim to total explanation'. Its ideology provides a *narrative* that 'promises to explain all historical happenings, the total explanation of the past, the total knowledge of the present, and the reliable prediction of the future'.[9] As a total explanation of the world, this ideology removes any experience of contingency.

The dataism of the information regime has totalitarian characteristics. Its aim is total knowledge, but the total knowledge of dataism is achieved not through ideological narration but through algorithmic *operations*. The aim of dataism is to *compute* all there is and all there will be. Big data does not recount. Recounting gives way to algorithmic counting. The information regime replaces all that is narrative with the numerical. However intelligent they may be, algorithms are not as effective as ideological narratives at excluding the possibility of the experience of contingency.

With totalitarianism, we bid farewell to the reality *given* to us by our five senses. Behind the given, totalitarianism constructs an *actual* reality, which requires a sixth sense. Dataism, by contrast, does not need a sixth sense. It does not transcend the *immanence of the given*, that is, the *data*. The literal meaning of the Latin *datum*, derived from *dare* (to give), is the *given*. Dataism does not paint a second reality behind the given, behind the data; it is a *totalitarianism without ideology*.

Totalitarianism creates obedient, amenable masses. Its ideology inspires the masses. The ideology breathes a *soul* into the masses. Gustave Le Bon, in his *The Crowd: A Study of the Popular Mind*, speaks of the soul of the masses that unifies the actions of masses. The information regime, by contrast, *isolates* people. When they come together, they form not a mass but a digital swarm; they follow not *one leader* but many influencers.

9

Electronic media is mass media in the sense that it creates mass man: '"Mass man" is the electronic occupant of the globe, simultaneously involved in all other people as if he were a spectator in a global ball park.'[10] Mass man has no identity – he is a 'nobody'.[11] Digital media brings the age of mass man to a close. The occupant of the digital globe is not a 'nobody'. He is a *someone with a profile* – in the age of the masses, the only people with profiles were criminals. By creating the individual's *behavioural profile*, the information regime ensnares him.

According to Walter Benjamin, the movie camera provides access to a special form of the unconscious: the 'optical unconscious'. Close-ups and slow motion render visible minute movements and actions that would have escaped the naked eye. An unconscious space appears: 'It is through the camera that we first discover the optical unconscious, just as we discover the instinctual unconscious through psychoanalysis.'[12] Benjamin's reflections on the optical unconscious can be applied to the information regime. Big data and artificial intelligence represent a *digital magnifying glass* through which is revealed an unconscious space, behind conscious activity, that is usually hidden to the actor. We may call it the *digital unconscious*. Big data and artificial intelligence enable the information regime to influence our behaviour at a level that lies below the threshold of consciousness. The information regime takes hold of those pre-reflexive, instinctual, emotive layers of behaviour that precede conscious actions. Its data-driven psychopolitics intervenes in our behaviour without us being aware of it.

Every shift towards a new major medium brings about a new regime of rule. *The medium is the form of rule.* Faced with the electronic revolution, Carl Schmitt felt that he needed to reformulate his famous definition of sovereignty: 'After the First World War, I said: "Sovereign is he who decides on the exception." After the Second World War, facing my death, I now say: "Sovereign is he who controls the waves in space."'[13] Digital media brings about the rule of information. The waves of the electronic mass media decline in importance. Power now depends on the possession of information. Domination is secured not by propaganda in the mass media but by information. In the face of the digital revolution, Schmitt would probably reformulate his statement on sovereignty yet again: *sovereign is he who has control over the information on the web.*

Infocracy

The digitalization of the lifeworld progresses inexorably. It is radically changing our perception, our relation to the world and our communal life. The frenzy of communication and information is stupefying. The tsunami of information is unleashing destructive forces. It has also taken hold of the world of politics, creating massive fault lines and disruptions in democratic processes. Democracy is degenerating into *infocracy*.

At the beginning of the democratic age, the book was the central medium. The book was what the rational discourse of the Enlightenment was based upon. The discursive public sphere, which is essential to democracy, was the result of a reasoning, reading public. In his *The Structural Transformation of the Public Sphere*, Jürgen Habermas points out that there is a close connection between the book and a democratic public:

From a reading public that consisted mainly of burgh-
ers [*Bürger*] and townspeople [*Stadtbürger*] and that was
larger than the republic of scholars . . . there emerged
from the centre of the private sphere, so to speak, a
comparatively dense network of public communication.[1]

Without the printing press, there would have been no
Enlightenment, no culture drawing on reason and on
reasoning. In a book-based culture, public discourse
is logically coherent: 'In a culture dominated by print,
public discourse tends to be characterized by a coherent,
orderly arrangement of facts and ideas.'[2]

The political discourse of the nineteenth century,
which was a book culture, was far more expansive and
complex than that of today. The famous public debates
between the Republican Abraham Lincoln and the
Democrat Stephen A. Douglas are a striking example. In
one debate, in 1854, Douglas first spoke for three hours.
Lincoln was given three hours for his reply, after which
Douglas spoke for another hour. Both speakers discussed
complex political facts, and used equally complex formu-
lations. The audience exhibited extraordinary powers of
concentration. For the audience, participation in public
discourse was a fixed element of social life.

Electronic mass media destroys the rational discourse
created by the book culture, producing a *mediacracy*.
Electronic mass media has a particular architectonic
design. Because of its amphitheatrical structure, its recipients are condemned to passivity. Habermas holds the
mass media responsible for the decay of the democratic
public sphere. Unlike a reading public, a television public
is at risk of being disenfranchised:

the programs sent by the new media curtail the reactions of their recipients in a peculiar way. They draw the eyes and ears of the public under their spell but at the same time, by taking away its distance, place it under 'tutelage', which is to say they deprive it of the opportunity to say something and to disagree. The critical discussion of a reading public tends to give way to 'exchanges about tastes and preferences' between consumers. . . . The world fashioned by the mass media is a public sphere in appearance only.[3]

In a mediacracy, politics submits to the logic of the mass media. The principle of amusement determines how political matters are conveyed, and undermines rationality. In his book *Amusing Ourselves to Death*, the American media theorist Neil Postman shows how infotainment leads to the decay of the power of judgement and plunges democracy into crisis. Democracy becomes telecracy. The highest priority is to provide entertainment, and this also becomes the priority in politics:

Efforts at gaining knowledge and being perceptive are removed by the business of distraction. As a consequence, we see a rapid decline of the human power of judgment. The business of distraction represents a clear threat: it makes people immature, or keeps them in a state of immaturity. And it corrodes the social foundation of democracy. We amuse ourselves to death.[4]

The news begins to take on the form of the story. The distinction between fiction and reality becomes blurred. Habermas also refers to infotainment's destructive effect on discourse: 'News and reports and even editorial opinions are dressed up with all the accoutrements of entertainment literature.'[5]

The mediacracy is also a *theatrocracy*. Politics is reduced to a series of staged events in the mass media. The election of an actor, Ronald Reagan, as president of the United States was the high point for mediacracy. What counts in televised debates is not the quality of the argument but the *performance*. The speaking time for presidential candidates is severely limited. They change the way they speak. The candidate with the better self-presentation wins the election. Discourse degenerates into show business and commercial slogans. Political substance becomes less and less important. Politics is hollowed out, reduced to telecratic image-politics.

Television fragments discourse. Even the print media takes its cue from TV: 'In the age of television, the paragraph is becoming the basic unit of news in print media. . . . the time cannot be far off when awards will be given for the best investigative sentence.'[6] Even though radio is well suited to the use of rational and complex language, it is not spared this process of disintegration. Its language becomes fragmented and discontinuous. In addition, the radio is under the thumb of the music industry. Its language is 'largely aimed at invoking visceral response' and becomes the 'linguistic analogue' of rock music.[7]

The history of domination can be cast in terms of different screens. Plato's cave allegory describes an archaic screen. The cave is built like a theatre. Behind the prisoners' backs, the jugglers perform their 'artistic tricks', with a fire casting the shadows of the jugglers' objects and figurines against the cave's wall. The prisoners, who have been tied up since childhood, stare only at the shadows and take them to be the sole reality. Plato's archaic screen illustrates the *dominion of myth*.

The so-called 'telescreen' plays a central role in Orwell's totalitarian surveillance state. It constantly shows propaganda. In front of it, the masses perform rituals of submission, chanting in a state of collective excitement. In private dwellings, the telescreen functions as a surveillance camera, and includes a very sensitive microphone that registers even the quietest of sounds. People live their lives believing that they are under constant surveillance by the Thought Police. The telescreens cannot be switched off. They are also biopolitical disciplinary apparatuses: every day, they deliver an exercise class that serves the purpose of producing docile bodies.

In a telecracy, Big Brother's surveillance screen is replaced with the television screen. People are not surveilled but entertained. They are not oppressed but turned into addicts. The Thought Police and the Ministry of Truth become superfluous. Instead of pain and torture, the means of domination are entertainment and amusement: 'In *1984* . . . people are controlled by inflicting pain. In *Brave New World*, they are controlled by inflicting pleasure. In short, Orwell feared that what we hate will ruin us. Huxley feared that what we love will ruin us.'[8]

In many respects, Huxley's *Brave New World* is closer to our present times than is Orwell's surveillance state. It is a *palliative society*. Pain is frowned upon, and intense feelings are repressed. Every wish and every need must be immediately satisfied. People are stupefied by fun, consumption and amusement. Their lives are dominated by the compulsion to be happy. The state distributes a drug called 'soma' to increase the feeling of happiness among the population. Instead of the telescreen, Huxley's *Brave New World* features cinemas providing 'feeling pictures', or 'feelies'. They include a 'scent organ' and deliver a whole-body experience that numbs people. Like soma, they are used as means of domination.

Today, telescreens and television screens have been replaced by touchscreens. The smartphone is the new medium of domination. Under the information regime, people are no longer passive spectators who surrender to amusement. They are all active transmitters. They constantly produce and consume information. Communication has become a form of addiction and compulsion, and the frenzy of communication ensures that people remain in a new state of immaturity. The information regime's formula for domination is: *we communicate ourselves to death.*

In *The Structural Transformation of the Public Sphere*, published in 1962, Habermas was only able to discuss electronic mass media. Today, digital media submits the public sphere to a radical structural change that would necessitate a fundamental revision of Habermas's thesis. In the age of digital media, the discursive public sphere is threatened not by the entertainment formats of mass media but by the viral spread and proliferation of information, that is, by an *infodemic.*[9] Digital media exhibits a centrifugal force that fragments the public sphere. The amphitheatrical structure of mass media gives way to the *rhizomatic structure* of digital media, which does not have a centre. The public sphere disintegrates into private spaces, and our attention is dispersed rather than directed towards issues relevant to all of society.

If we are to gain a deeper understanding of infocracy, of the democratic crisis under the information regime, we need a phenomenology of information. The democratic crisis begins at the cognitive level. Information is relevant only fleetingly. Because it lives off the 'appeal of surprise', information lacks *temporal stability*, and because of its temporal instability, it fragments our perception.[10] It draws reality into a 'permanent frenzy of actuality'.[11] It is not possible to *linger* on information. This makes the cognitive system restless. The compulsion towards acceleration inherent in information means that time-intensive cognitive practices such as *knowledge, experience* and *insight* are pushed aside.

Because of its fleeting relevance, information pulverizes time. Time disintegrates into a mere sequence of point-like presences. In this respect, information differs from narration, which generates temporal continuity. Today, time is fragmented on every level. The *temporal architectures* that *support* and stabilize life and perception are increasingly being eroded. The generally short-term nature of the information society is not conducive to democracy. Discourse is characterized by a temporality that is incompatible with accelerated, fragmented communication. Discourse is a time-intensive practice.

Rationality is also time-intensive. Rational decisions require a long-term perspective. They are based on reflections that extend beyond the present moment into both past and future. This temporal expansion characterizes rationality. In the information society, we simply do not have the time for rational action. The compulsion of accelerated communication deprives us of *rationality*. Under temporal pressure, we instead opt for *intelligence*.

18

Intelligence has a totally different temporality. Intelligent action aims at *short-term solutions and successes*. Luhmann rightly remarks: 'In an information society it is no longer possible to speak of rational behaviour. At best it is intelligent.'[12]

Discursive rationality is today under threat from affective communication. We allow ourselves to be easily *affected* by fast sequences of information. It is quicker to appeal to affect than to rationality. In affective communication, it is not the better argument but the most exciting information that prevails. Fake news is more interesting than fact. A single tweet containing fake news or a fragment of decontextualized information may be more effective than a reasoned argument.

Trump, the first Twitter president, fragmented his politics into tweets. His politics is determined not by a vision but by viral information. Infocracy promotes success-oriented, instrumental forms of action and leads to the spread of opportunism. The American mathematician Cathy O'Neil observes correctly that Trump acts like a perfectly opportunistic algorithm that takes only the reactions of the audience into account.[13] Temporally stable convictions or principles are sacrificed in favour of *quick and short-lived power gains*.

Psychometrics, also called psychographics, is a data-driven method for establishing a personality profile. When it comes to predicting a person's behaviour, psychometric profiling outperforms even that person's friends or partner. Given sufficient data, it is even possible to generate information that goes beyond what we believe we know about ourselves. A smartphone is a psychometric recording device that we feed daily, even hourly, with data. It makes possible the precise calculation of its user's personality. All the disciplinary regime had at its disposal was *demographic* information, which made possible its biopolitics. The information regime, by contrast, has access to *psychographic* information, which it uses for its psychopolitics.

Psychometrics is an ideal tool for psychopolitical marketing in politics. So-called micro-targeting makes use of psychometric profiling. Voters are sent personalized advertisements, based on their psychograms, via social media. Like consumer behaviour, voting behaviour is subjected to unconscious influences. Data-driven infocracy undermines the democratic process, which requires autonomy and freedom of the will. After Donald Trump's election victory in 2016, the British data analysis company Cambridge Analytica triumphantly declared: 'We are thrilled that our revolutionary approach to data-driven communications played such an integral part in President-elect Donald Trump's extraordinary win.'[14]

Micro-targeting does not inform voters about a party's political programme. Instead, voters receive manipulative electoral advertisements, and often fake news, based on their psychograms. Thousands of variations of an advertisement are tested for their efficiency. These psychometrically optimized *dark ads* represent a danger to democracy. Everyone receives a different message; the public is thus fragmented. Different groups receive different, often even contradictory, information. Citizens no longer pay attention to topics that are relevant to all of society. Instead, they are disenfranchised, treated as *voting cattle* to be manipulated in order to get politicians into power. *Dark ads* contribute to the division and polar-

20

ization of society and poison the discursive atmosphere. They are invisible to the public and thereby unhinge one of the fundamental principles of democracy: *society's self-observation.*

Today, anyone with access to the internet can create their own informational channels. Digital information technology reduces the production costs for information to practically nil. A Twitter account or YouTube channel can be created with a few movements of the hand. In the age of mass media, by contrast, the production costs for information were dramatically higher. Establishing a news channel is a laborious process. Accordingly, a mass media society lacks the infrastructure necessary for the mass production of fake news. Television may be a realm of illusion, but it is not yet a factory for fake news. Telecratic mediacracy is based on show and entertainment, not on false news and disinformation. The structural conditions for the infocratic disruption of democracy arrive only with the digital network.

Mediacracy reduces the electoral battle to a *war over the most successful performance* in the mass media. Rather than engage in discourse, politicians seek to put on an attractive show. Television, as the main medium of mediacracy, functions as a political stage. In infocracy, by contrast, the electoral battle degenerates into an *information war.* Twitter is *not a mediacratic stage but an infocratic arena.* Trump is not interested in delivering a good performance. He is leading a merciless information war.

Information wars are today waged using all conceivable technological and psychological means. In the US and Canada, voters are deluged with false news through automated phone messages. Armies of internet trolls intervene in electoral battles by systematically distributing fake news and conspiracy theories. Social bots – automated accounts on social media that pretend to be real people – post, tweet, like and share. They disseminate fake news and hate-filled comments; they rabble-rouse. In this way, citizens are replaced with robots. At zero marginal cost, these robots create voices (*Stimmen*) that produce a mood (*Stimmung*) and thus severely disfigure the political debate. They artificially increase the numbers of followers for certain accounts, thereby giving certain opinions the appearance of power. The tweets and comments of these bots steer the climate of opinion on social media in particular directions. Studies show that just a small number of bots can turn the climate of opinion around. They may not directly influence voter decisions, but they manipulate the environment in which the decisions are made. Voters are influenced without being aware of it. When politicians heed the mood on social media, political decisions are therefore being indirectly influenced by social media bots. And if citizens interact with opinion-manufacturing robots and allow themselves to be manipulated by them, if actors whose backgrounds and motivations remain hidden intervene in political debates, democracy is endangered. When an electoral battle takes the form of an information war, it is not the better argument but the more intelligent algorithm that prevails. In an infocracy, in this information war, discourse has no place.

In an infocracy, information is a weapon. The website of the well-known American right-wing radical and conspiracy theorist Alex Jones is tellingly called Infowars. Jones is a prominent representative of infocracy. His crude conspiracy theories and fake news reach an audience of millions, and those millions believe him. He presents himself as an 'infowarrior' fighting against the political establishment. Jones was among those who Donald Trump explicitly thanked for helping him to election victory in 2016. Information wars fought with fake news and conspiracy theories are symptomatic of a state of democracy in which truth and truthfulness are no longer of any importance. Democracy is disappearing into an impenetrable jungle of information.

So-called memes play a central role in election battles fought as information wars. Memes are comic drawings with short, provocative slogans, montaged photographs or short videos that go viral on social media. Following Donald Trump's election victory, the *Chicago Tribune* quoted a user of the internet forum 4chan: 'We actually elected a meme as president.'[15] CNN called the election of 2020 a 'meme election'. The electoral battle was 'the great meme war'. Some spoke of 'memetic warfare'.

Memes are online media viruses that spread at high speed, reproduce and mutate. The core information – the meme's RNA, so to speak – is planted in an infectious visual shell. Because memes aim primarily to trigger affects, meme-based viral communication makes rational discourse more difficult. The phenomenon of meme wars indicates that digital communication is increasingly visual rather than textual. After all, it takes much less time to take in an image than to read a text. Discourse and truth do not go viral. Because images do not present arguments or provide justifications, the increasing visualization of communication is an additional impediment to democratic discourse.

Democracy is a slow and drawn-out process. It takes time. For this reason, the viral spread of information, the *infodemic*, is particularly damaging to the democratic process. Arguments and justifications cannot be packed into a tweet or meme that spreads and multiplies with viral speed. The logical coherence that characterizes discourse is alien to viral media. Information follows its own logic, has its own temporality – it has its *own dignity beyond truth and lie*. Fake news is *first of all information*. It produces its *effect* before the process of verification has even begun. Information flies past the truth, and truth can never catch up. Any attempt at fighting the infodemic with truth is therefore doomed to fail. The infodemic is *resistant to truth*.

The End of Communicative Action

In his book *Collective Intelligence*, the media theorist Pierre Lévy paints a picture of a digital democracy that would be more direct than direct democracy. This kind of democracy is meant to *liquefy* frozen representative democracy by way of increased communication and constant feedback. It resembles the idea behind LiquidFeedback, software that was used for opinion formation and decision-making by the now insignificant Pirate Party and its surrounding circles: 'real-time democracy initiates a period of decision-making and continuous evaluation in which a responsible collective knows that it will eventually be confronted with the results of its current decisions'.[1] Instead of representation, which creates distance, it uses immediate participation. Real-time digital democracy is a *democracy of presence*. The smartphone becomes a *mobile parliament*, a forum for debate in any place and at any time. Real-time democracy, this dream of the early days of digitalization, is in fact an illusion. A digital swarm is not a responsible collective that can act politically. Instead, followers are trained by smart influencers and become consumer cattle. They are de-politicized. Algorithm-controlled communication on social media is neither free nor democratic. It brings about a new kind of immaturity. The smartphone is not a mobile parliament but an apparatus of subjugation. Because smartphones serve as *mobile shop windows* through which private matters are constantly presented to others, they accelerate the disintegration of the public sphere. They are much more likely to produce consumption and communication zombies than mature citizens.

Digital communication redirects information flows in a way that undermines the democratic process. Information is distributed without passing through public spaces. It is produced in private spaces and is sent to private spaces. The internet is therefore not a public sphere. Social media intensifies this *communication without community*. Influencers and followers do not add up to a political public sphere. Digital communities are commodified forms of community. In reality they are *commodities*. They are incapable of *acting politically*.

Digital networks lack the amphitheatrical structure of conventional mass media, which selects topics that are relevant to all of society and directs the attention of the whole population towards them. Because of the centrifugal forces inherent to digital networks, the public sphere disintegrates into a variety of swarms, each pursuing a particular interest. As communicative action requires large-scale public spheres, this makes communicative action harder.

The contemporary crisis of communicative action is also caused by social processes separate from the digital transformation of the public sphere. According to Hannah Arendt, political thinking is 'representative' in the sense that it involves making 'present to my mind the standpoints of those who are absent'. Representation, the presence of the other in opinion formation, is constitutive of democracy as a discursive practice: 'I form an opinion by considering a given issue from different viewpoints, by making present to my mind the standpoints of those who are absent; that is, I represent them.'[2] Democratic discourse requires the *power of the imagination*, of 'being and thinking in my own identity where actually I am not', and forming my opinion with the standpoints of other people in mind.[3] The process of reflection that leads to the formation of an opinion, Arendt says, is 'truly discursive' insofar as it is mindful of the *position of the other*. Without the *presence of the other*, my opinion is not discursive or representative but self-absorbed, doctrinal and dogmatic.

The *presence of the other* is also constitutive of Habermas's concept of communicative action:

> The concept of communicative action requires us to consider actors also as speakers and hearers who refer to something in the objective, social or subjective world, and mutually make validity claims that can either be accepted or disputed. Actors no longer refer *directly* to something in the objective, social or subjective world. Rather, they qualify their statements about something in the world in light of the possibility that they may be disputed by other actors.[4]

Proceeding *directly*, or *straight on*, is not a discursive movement. It is *discourse-blind*. Discourse is a *to and fro* movement. The Latin *discursus* means *walking around*. In discourse, we are – in a positive sense – distracted from our own convictions *by the other*. My statement or opinion acquires a discursive quality only through the *voice of the other*. Under conditions of communicative action, I need to be aware that what I say may be challenged by others. A statement that does not have a question mark hanging over it does not have a discursive character.

On a meta-level, our crisis of communicative action can be explained by the fact that *the other is disappearing*. The disappearance of the other means the end of discourse. It robs opinions of their communicative rationality. The expulsion of the other strengthens the auto-propagandistic compulsion to indoctrinate oneself with one's own ideas. This self-indoctrination produces self-referential info bubbles, which impede communicative action. With the development of the auto-propagandistic compulsion, dis-cursive spaces are increasingly replaced by echo chambers in which the only voice one hears is one's own.

Discourse presupposes that I can distinguish between my opinion and my identity. People who do not have this discursive ability hold fast to their opinions because they feel that their identities are threatened. Any attempt to persuade them to adopt a different opinion is therefore doomed to fail. They do not follow the *other*; they *do not listen*. Discourse, however, is a *practice of listening*. The crisis of democracy is first and foremost a *crisis of listening*.

According to Eli Pariser, the public sphere is being destroyed by the algorithmic personalization of the internet:

The new generation of Internet filters looks at the things you seem to like – the actual things you've done, or the things people like you like – and tries to extrapolate. They are prediction engines, constantly creating and refining a theory of who you are and what you'll do and want next. Together, these engines create a unique universe of information for each of us – what I've come to call a filter bubble – which fundamentally alters the way we encounter ideas and information.[5]

The longer I surf the internet, the more my filter bubble becomes filled with information that I like and that reinforces my convictions. I am shown only those views of the world that conform to my own. All other information is kept outside the bubble. In the filter bubble, I am caught in an endless 'you loop'.[6]

Eli Pariser considers the personalization of the internet a direct threat to democracy. Socially relevant topics that lie outside the sphere of immediate self-interest are, Pariser says, the 'bedrock and raison d'être of democracy'.[7] The personalization of the internet shrinks and limits our lifeworld and our experiential horizon, and in this way leads to the disintegration of democracy: 'In the filter bubble, the public sphere – the realm in which common problems are identified and addressed – is just less relevant.'[8]

The central weakness of the filter bubble theory is that it explains the narrowing of the experiential horizon that takes place in information society exclusively with reference to the algorithmic personalization of the internet. However, the disintegration of the public sphere is *not a purely technical problem*. The personalization of searches and newsfeeds makes only a small contribution to this

29

process of disintegration. Self-indoctrination or auto-propagandizing begins *offline*.

We are becoming deaf to the *voice of the other* because society is increasingly atomized and narcissistic. This also leads to a *loss of empathy*. Today, everyone buys into the cult of the self. Everyone stages and produces themselves. It is the *disappearance of the other*, the *inability to listen*, and not the algorithmic personalization of the internet that is responsible for the crisis of democracy.

A discursive situation oriented towards reaching understanding does not exist without a wider context. It is surrounded by a horizon of social practices and things taken for granted in a particular culture. This horizon pre-reflexively determines communicative action. Habermas calls this horizon of shared interpretative patterns the 'lifeworld'. The lifeworld forms a background consensus that stabilizes communicative action:

> Insofar as speakers and hearers straightforwardly achieve a mutual understanding about something in the world, they move within the horizon of their common life-world; this remains in the background of the participants – as an intuitively known, unproblematic, and unanalyz-able, holistic background. The speech situation is the segment of a lifeworld tailored to the relevant theme; it both forms a *context* and furnishes *resources* for the process of mutual understanding. The lifeworld forms a horizon and at the same time offers a store of things taken for granted in the given culture.[9]

An intact lifeworld is possible only in a relatively homogeneous society, with shared values and a shared cultural tradition. Globalization, and the *hyperculturalization* of society to which it leads, dissolves the cultural and traditional contexts that ground us in a shared lifeworld.[10] There are no longer any conventional identities with pre-reflexive validity. We are no longer *thrown* into a lifeworld that we take for granted and perceive as simply given. The lifeworld is now a *project* (*eine Frage des Entwurfes*). The holistic horizon that was once perceived as an inseparable unity is subjected to a radical process of fragmentation. In addition to globalization, digitalization and the creation of networks accelerate the disintegration of the lifeworld. The growing *defacticization* and *decontextualization* of the lifeworld destroy the 'holistic background' of communicative action. The disappearance of facticity in the lifeworld is a serious impediment to communication aimed at reaching understanding.

The defacticization of the lifeworld leads to calls for the establishment of internet spaces that make the experience of identity and community possible again. The idea is to create an *internet-based* lifeworld that is experienced as taken for granted and simply given – in other words, to *tribalize* the internet. The tribalization of the internet is particularly widespread on the political right where there is a greater need for identities that are anchored in a lifeworld – liberal cosmopolitans seem to do without it. On the right, even conspiracy theories are taken up as markers of *identity*. Digital tribes allow for deep experiences of identity and belonging. In such tribes, information is *not a source of knowledge but a source of identity*.[11] Conspiracy theories are particularly well suited to the creation of tribal biotopes on the internet because they allow for delimitation and exclusion, the mechanisms that constitute tribalism and its identity politics.

Tribal delimitation and isolation are not the result of an algorithmic personalization of the internet. They cannot be traced to the effects of filter bubbles. Digital tribes isolate themselves by *independently* selecting and using information for their identity politics. Contrary to the claims of the filter bubble theory, digital tribes are in fact confronted, inside their bubbles, with information that runs counter to their convictions. But this information is simply ignored, because it does not fit with the identity-creating narrative, and because to give up convictions would amount to a loss of identity that must be avoided at all costs. This is why tribal identity collectives reject any kind of discourse or dialogue. Reaching an understanding becomes impossible. The opinions the tribes express are not discursive but *sacred*: they fully coincide with their identities, which they will not give up under any circumstances.

Under conditions of communicative action, every participant makes a validity claim. If this claim is not accepted by the others, there will be a discourse. A discourse is a communicative act that attempts to reach an understanding in the face of differing validity claims. It takes place with the help of arguments that seek to justify or reject the validity claims. The rationality inherent in this kind of discourse is called *communicative rationality*.

The validity claimed by digital tribes and identity collectives is not discursive. It is an absolute claim, because it lacks communicative rationality. Communicative rationality depends on certain rules. It presupposes that opinions can be criticized as well as justified: 'An expression satisfies the precondition for rationality if and insofar as it embodies fallible knowledge and therewith has a relation to the objective world (that is, a relation to the facts) and is open to objective judgment.'[12] In the post-factual universe of digital tribes, expressions have lost their relation to facts. They lack any rationality. They cannot be criticized, nor is there a need to justify them with reasons. However, *committing oneself* to certain opinions gives one a feeling of *belonging*. Discourse is thus replaced with *belief* and *confession*. Outside of one's tribe, there are only enemies, *others* who must be fought. The tribalism of both right-wing and left-wing identity politics divides and polarizes society. It turns identity into a protective shield or fortress that repels any kind of otherness. The progressive tribalization of society is a threat to democracy. It leads to a *dictatorship of tribal opinion and identity* from which communicative rationality is absent.

As we lose the *dimension of the other*, so we lose the discursive dimension of communication. Society disintegrates into *irreconcilable identities without alterity*. Instead of discourse, we have *identity wars*. As a result, society loses what is held in common; it even loses its public spirit. *We no longer listen to each other. Listening* is a political act insofar as it is what brings people together as a community in the first place and makes discourse possible. It founds a *we*. A democracy is a *community of listeners*. Digital communication – that is, *communication without community* – *destroys the politics of listening*. We end up hearing only our own voices. That is the end of communicative action.

Digital Rationality

Dataists believe that the disintegration of the public sphere, the sheer amount of information and the rapidly increasing complexity of the information society make communicative action obsolete:

> 21st-century society is too complex, and thanks to information technology that complexity is made *all too plainly visible as is*. To borrow Herbert Simon's concept, the information to be processed became so substantial that it went beyond the 'bounded rationality' of individuals. Hence communication among people suffers paralysis on a daily basis, making it difficult for Arendt and Habermas' presuppositions to come into effect in reality. . . . In starting a discussion, citizens in contemporary society are not able to believe in a shared space for discussion. They cannot even share in the consciousness

of a point of departure that everyone is participating in a discussion, for the time being, as members of the same community. The public sphere that Arendt and Habermas held as an ideal is not activated to begin with.[1]

Faced with the erosion of communicative action, Habermas openly confesses that he is at a loss:

> I simply do not know what the equivalent to the communicative structures of the large-scale political public sphere that emerged since the eighteenth century should look like in the digital world. . . . How is it possible to maintain, in the virtual world of the decentred internet . . . a public sphere in which communication circulates so that it *includes all* of the population?[2]

Dataists seek a radical solution. They paint a picture of a kind of rationality that can do without communicative action. For them, big data and artificial intelligence are *functionally equivalent* to the discursive public sphere that is currently disintegrating, and this equivalence means that Habermas's theory of communicative action is obsolete. Discourse is replaced by data. The algorithmic processing of big data aims to capture and include the whole population. Dataists would even claim that artificial intelligence is a *better listener* than a human being.

We may call the kind of rationality that does without communication and discourse *digital rationality*. Its opposite is the communicative rationality that guides discourse. Communicative rationality crucially involves providing reasons, and also being prepared to learn. Habermas writes:

In virtue of their criticizability, rational expressions also admit of improvement; we can correct failed attempts if we can successfully identify our mistakes. The concept of *grounding* is interwoven with that of *learning*. Argumentation plays an important role in learning processes as well. Thus we call a person rational who, in the cognitive-instrumental sphere, expresses reasonable opinions and acts efficiently; but this rationality remains accidental if it is not coupled with the ability to learn from mistakes, from the refutation of hypotheses and from the failure of interventions.[3]

Artificial intelligence does not reason; it computes. In place of argument, there are algorithms. In the course of the discursive process, arguments can be *improved*. In the course of the computing process, algorithms are constantly *optimized*. They thereby independently correct the mistakes they make. Digital rationality replaces discursive learning with *machine learning*. In this way, algorithms imitate arguments.

From the perspective of the dataist, discourse is merely a slow, inefficient form of information processing, and the validity claims advanced by participants in a discourse are the products of insufficient information processing. Communicative action, dataists would argue, is only possible where, because of the inability of human understanding to process large amounts of information, there is limited information. Digitalization, however, *creates more information* than any discursive framework can capture.

Dataists believe that big data and artificial intelligence make possible an all-encompassing, divine gaze that can precisely capture all social processes and optimize them for the benefit of all. In his book *Social Physics: How Social Networks Can Make Us Smarter*, Alex Pentland, the director of the Human Dynamics Lab at MIT and a card-carrying dataist, writes:

> Big data give us a chance to view society in all its complexity, through the millions of networks of person-to-person exchanges. If we had a 'god's eye', an all-seeing view, then we could potentially arrive at a true understanding of how society works and take steps to fix our problems.[4]

Discourse guided by human understanding pales beside the god's-eye view of big data. Total digital knowledge makes discourse superfluous. Against Habermas's theory of communicative action, dataists advance a *behaviourist theory of information* that can do without discourse. In the dataist worldview, there are no rational actors who advance validity claims and defend them with argument.

Data mining, big data and artificial intelligence can find solutions to the problems and conflicts of a society that is understood as a predictable social system. These solutions are seen as beneficial to all members of society, who, because of their limited information-processing capacities, would not be able to find these solutions themselves. Big data and artificial intelligence therefore make more intelligent, even *more rational*, decisions than humans, who have a limited ability to process large quantities of information. From the dataist perspective, digital rationality is far superior to communicative rationality.

Dataists are convinced that, for the first time in its history, humanity has all the data needed to arrive at total knowledge of society. They promise us a world without war or financial crises, in which infectious diseases are quickly detected and eliminated. In 2014, Pentland wrote that only data could avoid mass death in the wake of a flu pandemic, and that only privacy concerns stood in the way of decisive progress along the path of civilization:

> The main barriers to achieving these goals are privacy concerns and the fact that we don't yet have any consensus around the trade-offs between personal and social values.
>
> We cannot ignore the public goods that such a sensory system could provide. Hundreds of millions of people could die in the next flu pandemic, and it appears that we now have the means to contain such disasters. Similarly, we are able not only to reduce energy use in cities dramatically, but . . . we can even shape cities and communities to both reduce crime and at the same time promote greater productivity and creative output.[5]

Dataists imagine a society that works *without any kind of politics*. They would argue that, if a social system is sufficiently stable, that is, if the system enjoys far-reaching consent at all social levels, then genuinely political action, action that aims to create new social conditions, is superfluous. When class-based conflicts and conflicts of interest abate, political parties become less important – and increasingly alike. Political parties and ideologies, dataists would argue, are only useful in a society in which systematic inequality, such as significant distributive injustice or class differences, is prevalent. From the dataist perspective, party-based democracy will soon no longer exist. It will give way to *infocracy, a digital post-democracy*. Politicians will be replaced with experts and computer scientists who will *administer* society without relying on ideological assumptions or advancing particular interests. Politics will be replaced by *data-driven systems management*, with decisions taken on the basis of big data and artificial intelligence. There will still be some political discourse, but it will be of secondary importance. More data and more intelligent algorithms – not more discourse and more communication – is what will allow us to optimize the social system, even to achieve the *happiness of all*.

Rousseau, enthused by the statistical methods developed in the eighteenth century, developed an *arithmetic rationality* that works without 'any communication' (*aucune communication*). It is the opposite of communicative rationality. Rousseau understands the general will (*volonté générale*) in terms of a purely mathematical variable that can be established objectively, without communicative action being involved. The general will is established by an arithmetic operation, that is, an algorithm, not by communication. In his *The Social Contract*, Rousseau says:

> There is often a great difference between the will of all (what all individuals want) and the general will; the general will studies only the common interest while the will of all studies private interest, and is indeed no more than the sum of individual desires. But if we take away from these same wills, the pluses and minuses which cancel each other out, the balance which remains is the general will.[6]

Rousseau explicitly points out that the general will must be established without 'any communication'– that it even has to exclude it. It is a condition for the possibility of establishing the general will that citizens 'do not have any communication among themselves': that there is no discourse. Every communication distorts the picture of the general will. Rousseau even prohibits political parties and associations because they eliminate 'differences' in order to further their interests. Everyone should hold on to their individual convictions and opinions instead of participating in a discourse, because otherwise

> The differences become less numerous and yield a result less general. Finally, when one of these groups becomes so large that it can outweigh the rest, the result is no longer the sum of many small differences, but one great divisive difference; then there ceases to be a general will, and the opinion which prevails is no more than a private opinion.
>
> Thus if the general will is to be clearly expressed, it is imperative that there should be no sectional associations in the state, and that every citizen should make up his own mind for himself.[7]

In the language of the dataists, Rousseau's thesis runs as follows: the more data there is, the less distorted is the general will that is computed. Discourse, by contrast, distorts the result. This makes Rousseau the first dataist. His arithmetic rationality, which avoids the need for discourse and communication, approaches digital rationality. Under the information regime, Rousseau's statisticians are replaced with computer experts. The general will, that is, 'the best for everyone' in a society, is to be established by artificial intelligence and big data.

Communicative rationality is based on the autonomy and freedom of the individual. Dataists, by contrast, advocate a digital behaviourism that discards the idea of the free, autonomous individual. As behaviourists, they are convinced that an individual's behaviour can be precisely predicted and controlled. Total knowledge renders the freedom of the individual obsolete:

> His abolition has long been overdue. Autonomous man is a device used to explain what we cannot explain in any other way. He has been constructed from our ignorance, and as our understanding increases, the very stuff of which he is composed vanishes. . . . To man qua man we readily say good riddance. Only by dispossessing him can we turn to the real causes of human behaviour. Only then can we turn from the inferred to the observed, from the miraculous to the natural, from the inaccessible to the manipulable.[8]

Where communicative rationality starts with the individual, digital rationality starts with the collective. From the dataist perspective, the autonomous actor is a fiction: 'It is time that we dropped the fiction of individuals as the unit of rationality, and recognised that our rationality is largely determined by the surrounding social fabric.'[9] Our behaviour follows the laws of social physics. Dataists believe that humans do not differ fundamentally from bees or apes:

41

the power of social physics comes from the fact that almost all of our day-to-day actions are habitual, based mostly on what we have learned from observing the behavior of others. ... This means that we can observe humans in just the same way we observe apes or bees and derive rules of behavior, reaction, and learning.[10]

Alex Pentland complements data mining with 'reality mining'. People are equipped with so-called 'sociometers', which record the minutiae of their behaviour down to the level of bodily expression, thus generating enormous volumes of behavioural data. 'Reality mining' through digital sensors promises to make society predictable and controllable:

In just a few short years we are likely to have incredibly rich data available about the behavior of virtually all of humanity – on a continuous basis. ... And once we develop a more precise visualization of the patterns of human life, we can hope to understand and manage our modern society in ways better suited to our complex, interconnected network of humans and technology.[11]

Dataists conceive of society as a functional organism. It differs from other organisms only in virtue of its higher level of complexity. In a society seen as an organism, there are no validity claims. There is no discourse between organs. The only thing that matters is an *efficient exchange of information* between functional units in order to increase performance. Politics and governments are replaced with planning, control and conditioning.

The behaviourist view of human beings cannot readily be made to agree with democratic principles. In the dataist universe, democracy gives way to a *data-driven infocracy* that seeks to optimize the exchange of information. The discursive public sphere is replaced by the analysis of data with the help of artificial intelligence, a process that ultimately spells the end of democracy. Shoshana Zuboff emphatically rejects the dataist vision of the human being:

> If democracy is to be replenished in the coming decades, it is up to us to rekindle the sense of outrage and loss over what is being taken from us. . . . What is at stake here is the human expectation of sovereignty over one's own life and authorship of one's own experience. What is at stake is the inward experience from which we form the will to will and the public spaces to act on that will.[12]

To the dataist ear, this passionate commitment to freedom and democracy will sound like a ghostly voice from an already bygone era. From the dataist perspective, the idea of the human being as defined by individual autonomy and freedom, by the 'will to will', will eventually appear as merely a short historical interlude. Dataists would agree with Foucault when he invokes the death of the human being in *The Order of Things*: 'As the archaeology of our thought easily shows, man is an invention of recent date. And one perhaps nearing its end. . . . then one can certainly wager that man would be erased, like a face drawn in sand at the edge of the sea.'[13] The sea whose waves are erasing the face in the sand is today a boundless sea of data, in which the human being dissolves into an insignificant data set.

The Crisis of Truth

A *new nihilism* is spreading. This nihilism is not a result of religious articles of faith or traditional values losing their validity. That *nihilism of values* which Nietzsche expressed when he said 'God is dead', or spoke of a 'trans-valuation of all values', we have already left behind. The new nihilism is a phenomenon of the twenty-first century. It is part of the *pathological fault lines of the information society*. This nihilism emerges when we lose faith in truth itself. In the age of fake news, disinformation and conspiracy theories, we are losing our sense of reality and its factual truths. The circulation of information is completely decoupled from reality; it takes place in a hyperreal space. The belief in *facticity* is lost. We therefore live in a *defacticized* universe. Ultimately, the loss of factual truth means the loss of a *shared world* as a framework for our actions.

Despite its radical nature, Nietzsche's critique of truth does not aim at the destruction of truth. It does not deny truth itself; it only uncovers its moral origins. Truth is de-*constructed*, that is, genealogically *reconstructed*. According to Nietzsche, truth is a social construction that serves the purpose of facilitating human communal life. It provides communal life with an existential foundation:

> *The drive for truth* begins with the keen observation of the opposition between the real world and the world of lies and how all human existence becomes uncertain if conventional truth is not unconditionally binding: it is a moral conviction about the necessity of a rigid convention if any human society is supposed to exist. If the *state of war* is ever to cease, then it must begin with the fixing of truth, that is, with a valid and binding *signification* of things.
>
> The liar uses words to make the unreal appear real, that is, he misuses the firm foundation.[1]

The concept of truth ensures that different validity claims do not lead to a *bellum omnium contra omnes*, to the *complete fracturing of society*. It is a necessary convention that holds society together.

Today, Nietzsche's critique of society would be even more radical. He would describe our total loss of the *drive for truth*, the *will to truth*. The drive for truth develops only in a society that is unbroken. The disappearance of the drive for truth and the disintegration of society cause each other. When a society disintegrates into groups or tribes between which no understanding is possible, which share no sense of the *binding signification of things*, the crisis of truth spreads. In the crisis, the shared world, even the shared language, is lost. Truth regulates social life, it is a regulative idea of society.

The new nihilism is a symptom of the information society. Truth contains a centripetal force that holds a society together, but information contains a centrifugal force that destroys social cohesion. The new nihilism emerges within the same destructive process that leads to the *crisis of democracy*: the *disintegration of discourse into information*.

The new nihilism does not mean that lies are presented as truths or truths discredited as lies. Rather, the distinction between truth and lie is undermined. Paradoxically, someone who intentionally lies and contradicts truth thereby acknowledges the truth. It is possible to lie only if the distinction between truth and lie is still intact. A liar does not lose his relation to truth. His faith in reality is not shaken. A liar is not a nihilist. He does not question truth itself. The more determined the lie, the more validated the truth.

Fake news is not a series of lies. Fake news is an attack on the facts themselves. It defacticizes reality. In asserting whatever suits his purposes, without compunction, Donald Trump is not a typical liar – someone who intentionally distorts things. He is, rather, indifferent towards factual truth. Someone who is blind to fact and reality poses a greater threat to truth than does a liar.

The American philosopher Harry Frankfurt would call Trump a 'bullshitter'. A bullshitter does not contradict the truth; he is completely indifferent to truth. Frankfurt's explanation for why there is so much bullshit today is, however, insufficient:

Bullshit is unavoidable whenever circumstances require someone to talk without knowing what he is talking about. Thus the production of bullshit is stimulated whenever a person's obligations or opportunities to speak about some topic exceed his knowledge of the facts that are relevant to that topic. . . . Closely related instances arise from the widespread conviction that it is the responsibility of a citizen in a democracy to have opinions about everything, or at least everything that pertains to the conduct of his country's affairs.[2]

If bullshit were the result of insufficient knowledge, Trump would not be a bullshitter. Harry Frankfurt does not seem to grasp today's crisis of truth. This crisis cannot be explained in terms of a discrepancy between knowledge and facts or a lack of knowledge of reality. The crisis of truth shakes belief in the facts themselves. Opinions 'can differ widely' but still be 'legitimate as long as they respect factual truth'.[3] Freedom of opinion degenerates into a farce, by contrast, if it loses all reference to facts and factual truth.

The erosion of truth began long before Trump's politics of fake news. In 2005, *The New York Times* declared the neologism 'truthiness' to be one of the words that have captured the zeitgeist. Truthiness reflects the crisis of truth. It means a felt truth that lacks any objectivity or factual solidity. Its subjective wilfulness, which is its essence, eliminates the truth. This wilfulness expresses the nihilistic attitude towards reality. It is a pathological phenomenon of digitalization. It does not belong to the book culture. The digital, in particular, erodes the factual. The television presenter Stephen Colbert, who coined the term truthiness, once remarked: 'I don't trust books. They're all fact, no heart.'[4] Trump, accordingly, would be a *president of the heart* who makes little use of understanding. The heart is not an organ of democracy. When emotions and affects dominate political discourse, democracy itself is in danger.

In her *The Origins of Totalitarianism*, Arendt writes:

> Hitler circulated millions of copies of his book in which he stated that to be successful, a lie must be enormous, that is, it must not be limited to a denial of individual facts within a factual context that remains intact (in which case this context will always eventually show the lies for what they are), but must replace the whole factual edifice so that the false facts of individual lies form a consistent context and put a fictional world in place of the real one.[5]

According to Arendt, Hitler was not a conventional liar. He was capable of a kind of lie whose *enormity* and *totality* produces a new reality. Someone who invents a new reality does not lie in the conventional sense.

The relationship between ideology and truth is, however, far more complex than Arendt assumes. Hitler, too, had a firm commitment to truth. He continued to regard truth as an authority. He spread his racist ideology in the name of truth. He always presented his propaganda in the light of truth. There are truths, Hitler wrote, that are 'so obvious that just for this reason the common world does not see, or at least does not recognize, them'. The world 'passes these well-known truisms blindly and it is most astonished if now somebody discovers what everybody ought to know'.[6] Truth is one of the concepts frequently used by Hitler in *Mein Kampf*. There are the 'guardians of a higher truth',[7] and there is talk of 'eternal truth'.[8] He distances himself from the 'promoters of lies and calumnies'[9] and presents himself as the herald of truth. The Jews, in particular, are defamed by him as 'the great masters of lying' and accused of living a lie: 'their entire existence is built on one single great lie'.[10]

The truth also retains its position of authority in Orwell's totalitarian surveillance state, which is erected on a monumental lie that presents itself as the truth. Winston Smith, the protagonist, says: 'And if all others accepted the lie which the Party imposed – if all records told the same tale – then the lie passed into history and became truth.'[11] The Party lies, but such is the enormity of the lie that it turns into truth. The Party continues to make use of the authority of truth. The Ministry of Truth plays a central role in Orwell's dystopian world. It is a 'enormous pyramidal structure of glittering white concrete, soaring up, terrace after terrace, 300 metres into the air'.[12] The building dominates the cityscape. It has 3,000 rooms. The Ministry of Truth is concerned 'with news, entertainment, education, and the fine arts'.[13] It provides the population with newspapers, films, music, theatre and books. It produces low-quality papers filled with crime and sports, cheap sensationalist novels and sentimental pop songs. Its aim is to prevent independent thought among the population. The Ministry of Truth even has a whole subdivision dedicated to the mass production of pornography. Porn is used as a means of domination. Someone who is addicted to porn or gaming will not revolt against the rulers.

The central function of the Ministry of Truth is the destruction of factual truth. The facticity of facts is annulled. By continuously bringing the past into harmony with the present, the past is erased. All documents are constantly revised and adapted to accord with the present party line, so that all written records confirm the Party's stance. The Ministry of Truth perfects the practice of the total lie. It does not simply disseminate individual pieces of *fake news*. Rather, it upholds a fictional reality at all costs. Facts are bent and fashioned into lies so that they conform to the party narrative that defines reality.

Winston's job in the Ministry of Truth is falsification. He replaces facts from the past that are not favourable to the Party's interests with invented facts. Having just made up a fictional person called Ogilvy in the course of rewriting a newspaper article, he tells himself: 'Comrade Ogilvy, who had never existed in the present, now existed in the past, and when once the act of forgery was forgotten, he would exist just as authentically, and upon the same evidence, as Charlemagne or Julius Caesar.'[14]

Universal deceit, total lying, also intervenes in the language itself. A new language, 'Newspeak', is invented. It solidifies the total lie. The vocabulary is radically reduced. Linguistic nuances are eradicated in order to prevent any subtlety of thought. People are deprived of the ability to conceive of a world that is different from that projected by the Party. The total lie bends language itself and turns it into lying. Clear conceptual distinctions are made impossible. The Party's three slogans are: 'War is peace. Freedom is slavery. Ignorance is strength.'[15]

Trump's fake news is not an enormous lie that creates a new reality. The word 'truth' hardly ever crosses Trump's lips. He does not lie in the name of truth. His alternative facts do not congeal into a narrative or ideological narration. They lack narrative continuity and coherence. Trump's politics of fake news is possible only under the conditions of a *de-ideologized information regime*.

Hannah Arendt was still convinced that factual truths are 'stubborn' and that their 'fragility is oddly combined with great resilience – the same irreversibility that is the hallmark of the results of all human action, as opposed to the results of human production'.[16] The stubbornness and resilience of facts is now a thing of the past.

In general, the digital order undermines the solidity of the factual, even the *solidity of being*, because it makes *producibility* universal. Under conditions of universal producibility, nothing is irreversible. The digital world, that is, the informationalized world, is anything but stubborn and resilient. It can be formed and manipulated at will. *The digital is directly opposed to factuality.* Digitalization weakens the sense of the factual, even the sense of reality. Universal producibility also characterizes digital photography. Analogue photography authenticates the *being* of what *there is*. For the viewer, it bears witness to the 'this-has-been'.[17] It shows us what *is factually there*. This-has-been, or such-a-thing-existed, is the *truth of photography*. Digital photography destroys *facticity as truth*. By eliminating reality as the referent, it *produces* a new reality that does *not exist*.

Information does not by itself explain the world. Beyond a certain point, it can even come to obscure the world. Confronted with information, we always suspect: it could be *otherwise*. All information is accompanied by a *basic distrust*. The more we are confronted with different pieces of information, the stronger the distrust becomes. In the information society, we lose our basic trust. The information society is a *society of distrust*.

The information society increases the experience of contingency. Information lacks the *solidity of being*: 'Its cosmology is a cosmology not of being but of contingency.'[18] Information is a Janus-faced concept. Like the sacred before it, it has 'a benedictory and a frightening side'. It leads to 'paradoxical communication' because it 'reproduces certainty and uncertainty'. Information produces a *fundamental structural ambivalence*. Luhmann says: 'Each moment, the fundamental ambivalent pattern takes new forms, but the ambivalence remains nevertheless. Is this, perhaps, what is meant when we speak of an "information society"?'[19]

Information is *additive* and *cumulative*. Truth, by contrast, is *narrative* and *exclusive*. There are heaps of information and junk information. But truth does not form heaps (*Haufen*). It does not *heap up* (*ist nicht häufig*). In many respects, truth is opposed to information. It eliminates contingency and ambivalence. When elevated to the form of a narrative, it provides meaning and orientation. The information society, by contrast, is devoid of meaning. Only *emptiness* is *transparent*. Today, we may be *well informed*, but we lack orientation. Information does not have the power to provide orientation. Even the most diligent fact-check cannot produce truth, because truth is more than the rightness or correctness of information. Truth, ultimately, is a *promise*, as Christ says: 'I am the way, the truth, and the life' (John 14:6).

Even Habermas's concept of discursive truth has a teleological dimension. It is the 'promise to reach a rational consensus about what is being said'.[20] Discourse is the 'process of argumentation' that decides on the truth content of claims.[21] The idea is that truth depends on the discursive confirmation of validity claims. In other words, the claims must withstand possible counter-arguments and elicit the consent of all potential participants in the discourse. Discursive truth, the process of reaching understanding and consensus, provides social cohesion. Because it eliminates contingency and ambivalence, it stabilizes society.

The crisis of truth is always a crisis of society. Without truth, society disintegrates *from within*, and this means it comes to be held together only by external, instrumental, economic relations. The currently widespread social practice of mutual evaluation, for instance, destroys human relations by submitting them to complete commercialization. All human values are commercialized and subjected to economic imperatives. Society and culture take on the commodity form. Commodities (*Ware*) replace truth (*das Wahre*).

Information and data do not by themselves *illuminate* the world. Their nature is transparency. *Light and darkness* are not properties of information. Like *good and evil* or *truth and lie*, light and darkness emerge in narrative space. Truth, in the proper sense, has a narrative character. In the de-narrativized information society, truth therefore radically declines in importance.

The end of grand narratives that heralded postmodernity culminates in the information society. *Narratives disintegrate into information*. Information is the opposite of narration. *Big* data is opposed to the *grand* narrative. Big data does not *narrate* anything. In French, 'digital' is '*numérique*'. The numerical and the narrative, the countable and the recountable, belong to two fundamentally different orders.

Conspiracy theories flourish particularly well in times of crisis. Today, we face not only an economic and health crisis but also a *narrative* crisis. Narrative provides meaning and identity, so the narrative crisis leads to a vacuum of meaning, an identity crisis and a lack of orientation. In this context, conspiracy theories, as *micro-narratives*, are a remedy. They are taken up as *resources that provide identity and meaning*. That is why they spread especially on the political right, where the need for identity is particularly strong.

Conspiracy theories resist attempts at fact-checking because they are narratives that, despite their fictional character, provide a basic framework through which their adherents perceive reality. In this way, they are factual narrations. In a conspiracy theory, fictionality turns into factuality. What matters is not factuality in the sense of the facticity of truth but the narrative coherence that makes the theory credible. The narrative of a conspiracy theory eliminates contingency. Contingency and complexity, which are experienced as particularly stressful during crises, are *narrated away* by the conspiracy theory. In the pandemic crisis, figures such as 'reported cases' or 'incidence' intensify the fundamental insecurity because they do not *explain* anything. *Counting* gives rise to a need for *recounting*. This makes the pandemic crisis a fertile soil for the growth of conspiracy theories. Their universal explanations, or universal lies, remove the stressful insecurity and uncertainty at a stroke.

Democracy and the new nihilism do not go together.

Democracy presupposes truthful speaking. In his last lecture, delivered shortly before his death, Michel Foucault, as if he had sensed the coming crisis of truth in which we are losing the *will to truth*, addressed the 'courage of the truth' (parrēsia). With reference to the Greek historian Polybius, Foucault points out that 'true democracy' is guided by two principles, *isegoria* and *parrēsia*. Isegoria is every citizen's right to free expression. Parrēsia, speaking the truth, presupposes isegoria but goes further than the constitutional right to speak up. It enables certain individuals to address themselves to others, 'to tell them what they think, what they think is true, what they truly think is true'.[22] Thus, parrēsia requires individuals who act politically to tell the truth, to care for the community by making 'use of discourse, but of rational discourse, the discourse of Truth'.[23] Someone who speaks up courageously, despite the risks it entails, practises parrēsia. Parrēsia founds community. It is essential to democracy. Speaking the truth is a genuinely political act. As long as parrēsia is practised, democracy is alive:

> I think . . . that this parrēsia . . . is first of all profoundly linked to democracy. . . . we can say that there is a sort of circular relation between democracy and parrēsia . . . In order for there to be democracy there must be parrēsia. But conversely . . . parrēsia is one of the characteristic features of democracy. It is one of the internal dimensions of democracy.[24]

Parrēsia, the courage of the truth, of the 'courageous parrhesiast', is the *political act par excellence*. True democracy therefore contains something *heroic*. It needs those people who dare to speak the truth despite all the risks involved. So-called freedom of expression, by contrast, concerns only isegoria. Only with the *freedom of truth* does real democracy emerge. Without this freedom, democracy approaches infocracy.

Politics is also a power game. The term *dunasteia* signifies the exercise of power, 'the game through which power is actually exercised in a democracy'.[25] However, in a democracy, dunasteia is not blind. It is not an end in itself. The power game has to take place within the framework of parrēsia. Parrēsia limits and constrains it. If the power game is played just for its own sake, democracy is in danger. Donald Trump, for instance, exemplifies political power that has lost all relation to parrēsia. As an opportunist, he is interested only in gaining ever more power. Fake news is a means to that end.

Parrēsia has degenerated into everyone's freedom to say whatever they please, whatever they like or whatever is advantageous to them. People do not hesitate to make claims that do not bear the slightest relationship to the facts. Plato's critique of democracy is aimed at this form of parrēsia. According to Plato, democracy ultimately produces a 'state bursting with freedom and frankness (*eleutheria* and *parrēsia*)', a 'state without unity', a 'motley and diverse city in which everyone gives their opinion, follows their own decisions, and governs himself as he likes'.[26] Today, democracy has reached this point. People claim whatever they will. This threatens the very unity of society.

Plato juxtaposes a parrēsia understood as the arbitrary assertion of opinions with a good and courageous parrēsia. The true parrhesiast differs from the populist or

56

politician who seeks to flatter the people. Speaking the truth is not without its dangers. Socrates, in particular, embodies courageous parrēsia. His speech always exhibits a *care for the truth*. His task is to speak the truth, and he pursues this task to his death. The task coincides with his existence as a philosopher. He accepts it even though it means the risk of death. Foucault puts a strong emphasis on Socrates' role as parrhesiast:

> We have here an example which proves that, in democracy, one risks death by wanting to speak the truth in favor of justice and the law. . . . It is true that parrhēsia is dangerous, but it is also true that Socrates had the courage to confront the risks of parrhēsia.[27]

Philosophy has now bade farewell to speaking the truth, to the *care for truth*. By calling philosophy 'a kind of radical journalism', and understanding himself as a 'journalist', Foucault committed himself and philosophy to speaking the truth.[28] Philosophy is speaking the truth. Philosophers, Foucault says, have to be uncompromising in their concern with the 'present'. They practise parrēsia with regard to what is going on *today*. When Hegel says that philosophy captures its time in thought, he also understands himself to be a journalist. The care for today, or care for truth, is ultimately concerned with the future: 'I think it is we [the philosophers] who make the future. The future is the way in which we react to what is happening, the way in which we transform a movement, a doubt, into truth.'[29] Today's philosophy lacks any relation to the truth. It turns away from the present. It is therefore also *without future*.

57

Plato embodies the *regime of truth*. In his allegory of the cave, one of the prisoners is led outside. The liberated prisoner sees the *light of truth* and returns to the cave in order to convince the others of the actual reality. He adopts the role of the parrhesiast, the philosopher. But the prisoners do not believe him, and they try to kill him. The allegory of the cave ends thus: 'And, as for anyone who tried to free them and lead them upward, if they could somehow get their hands on him, wouldn't they kill him? – They certainly would.'[30]

Today, thinking ourselves free, we are in fact captives in a *digital* cave. We are tied to the digital screen. The prisoners in Plato's cave are intoxicated by mythic and narrative images. The digital cave, by contrast, holds us *captive in information*. The *light of truth* has died down completely. The cave of information has no *outside*. The loud *buzz of information* blurs the *contours of being. Truth does not buzz.*

The temporality of truth is completely different from that of information. While information is relevant only very briefly, truth is characterized by *duration*. It stabilizes life. Hannah Arendt explicitly emphasizes the existential significance of truth. Truth gives us *something to hold on to*: 'it is the ground on which we stand and the sky that stretches above us'.[31] Earth and sky belong to the terrestrial order, which has today been eliminated by the digital order. Arendt still lived in the terrestrial order. For her, truth possesses the *stability of being*. In the digital order, this stability gives way to the *fleetingness of information*. We will probably have to make do with information. The *age of truth* appears to be over. The regime of information has supplanted the regime of truth.

In a totalitarian state that is built on a universal lie, speaking the truth is a revolutionary act. The parrhesiast has the *courage of the truth*. In the post-factual world of the information society, by contrast, the urgency of truth completely evaporates. It is lost amid the buzz of information. Truth collapses into informational dust, which is blown away by the digital wind. The reign of truth will turn out to have been a brief one.

Notes

The Information Regime

1 Michel Foucault, *Discipline and Punish: The Birth of the Prison*, New York: Vintage, 1995, p. 135.

2 Ibid., p. 136.

3 Ibid., p. 237 (transl. modified).

4 Michel Foucault, 'The Birth of Social Medicine', in *Essential Works of Foucault 1954–1984: Vol. 3, Power*, ed. James D. Faubion, New York: The New Press, 2000, pp. 134–56; here: p. 137.

5 Foucault, *Discipline and Punish*, p. 217.

6 Ibid., p. 187.

7 Ibid., p. 201.

8 Vilém Flusser, *Dinge und Undinge: Phänomenologische Skizzen*, Munich: Hanser, 1993, p. 87.

9 Hannah Arendt, *The Origins of Totalitarianism*, London: André Deutsch, 1986, p. 470.

10 Marshall McLuhan and Barrington Nevitt, 'The

Electronic World Affects Identity Images', *Modern Office Procedures* (December 1975), pp. 12–16; here: p. 16.

11 Ibid.

12 Walter Benjamin, 'The Work of Art in the Age of Its Technological Reproducibility', in *The Work of Art in the Age of Its Technological Reproducibility and Other Writings on Media*, Cambridge, MA: Harvard University Press, 2008, pp. 19–55; here: p. 37.

13 Quoted after Christian Linder, *Der Bahnhof von Finnentrop: Eine Reise ins Carl Schmitt Land*, Berlin: Matthes & Seitz, 2008, p. 423.

Infocracy

1 Jürgen Habermas, *Strukturwandel der Öffentlichkeit: Untersuchungen zu einer Kategorie der bürgerlichen Gesellschaft*, Frankfurt am Main: Suhrkamp, 1990, p. 13 (from the preface to the German edition of 1990, which is not contained in the English edition).

2 Neil Postman, *Amusing Ourselves to Death: Public Discourse in the Age of Show Business*, London: Penguin, 2006 [1985], p. 51.

3 Jürgen Habermas, *The Structural Transformation of the Public Sphere: An Inquiry into a Category of Bourgeois Society*, Cambridge: Polity, 1992, p. 171.

4 Neil Postman, *Wir amüsieren uns zu Tode: Urteilsbildung im Zeitalter der Unterhaltungsindustrie*, Frankfurt am Main: Fischer, 1988, p. 2 (German publisher's note).

5 Habermas, *The Structural Transformation of the Public Sphere*, p. 170.

6 Postman, *Amusing Ourselves to Death*, p. 112.

7 Ibid.

8 Ibid., p. xx.

9 As early as mid-February 2020, the director-general of the World Health Organization, Tedros Adhanom

Ghebreyesus, said: 'We're not just fighting an epidemic; we're fighting an infodemic.' See https://twitter.com /WHO/status.

10 Niklas Luhmann, 'Entscheidungen in der "Informations-gesellschaft"', at https://www.fen.ch/texte/gast_luhmann _informationsgesellschaft.htm.

11 Robert Feustel, *Am Anfang war die Information: Digitalisierung als Religion*, Berlin: Verbrecher, 2018, p. 150.

12 Luhmann, 'Entscheidungen in der "Informations-gesellschaft"'.

13 See https://www.huffpost.com/entry/donald-trump-is-like-a-biased-machine-learning-algorithm_b_11524300.

14 See https://www.prnewswire.com/news-releases/cambrid ge-analytica-congratulates-president-elect-donald-trump -and-vice-president-elect-mike-pence-300359987.html.

15 See https://www.chicagotribune.com/business/blue-sky/ ct-meme-president-4chan-trump-wp-bsi-20161112-story. html.

The End of Communicative Action

1 Pierre Lévy, *Collective Intelligence: Mankind's Emerging World in Cyberspace*, New York: Basic Books, 1997, pp. 80f.

2 Hannah Arendt, 'Truth and Politics', in *Between Past and Future: Eight Exercises in Political Thought*, New York: Viking Press, pp. 227–64; here: p. 241.

3 Ibid.

4 Jürgen Habermas, 'Erläuterungen zum Begriff des kommunikativen Handelns (1982)', in *Vorstudien und Ergänzungen zur Theorie des kommunikativen Handelns*, Frankfurt am Main: Suhrkamp, 1995 [1984], pp. 571–606; here: p. 588.

5 Eli Pariser, *The Filter Bubble: What the Internet Is Hiding from You*, London: Penguin, 2011, p. 9.

6 Ibid., p. 109.
7 Ibid., p. 75.
8 Ibid., p. 148.
9 Jürgen Habermas, *The Philosophical Discourse of Modernity*, Cambridge: Polity, 1987, p. 298.
10 See Byung-Chul Han, *Hyperculture: Culture and Globalization*, Cambridge: Polity, 2022.
11 See Michael Seemann, 'Digitaler Tribalismus und Fake News', at https://www.ctrl-verlust.net/digitaler -tribalismus-und-fake-news.
12 Jürgen Habermas, *The Theory of Communicative Action*, *Vol. 1*, Cambridge: Polity, 1986, p. 9.

Digital Rationality

1 Hiroki Azuma, *General Will 2.0: Rousseau, Freud, Google*, New York: Vertical, 2014, pp. 68f.
2 Jürgen Habermas, 'Moralischer Universalismus in Zeiten politischer Regression: Jürgen Habermas im Gespräch über die Gegenwart und sein Lebenswerk', *Leviathan* 48 (1), 2020, pp. 7–28; here: p. 27.
3 Habermas, *The Theory of Communicative Action, Vol. 1*, p. 18.
4 Alex Pentland, *Social Physics: How Social Networks Can Make Us Smarter*, London: Penguin, 2015, p. 11.
5 Ibid., p. 106.
6 Jean-Jacques Rousseau, *The Social Contract*, London: Penguin, 1968, pp. 72f.
7 Ibid., p. 73.
8 B. F. Skinner, *Beyond Freedom and Dignity*, London: Penguin, 1973, p. 196.
9 Alex Pentland, 'The Death of Individuality: What Really Governs your Actions?', *New Scientist*, vol. 222, 2014, pp. 30f.; here: p. 31.
10 Pentland, *Social Physics*, p. 127.

11 Ibid. p. 24.

12 Shoshana Zuboff, *The Age of Surveillance Capitalism: The Fight for a Human Future at the New Frontier of Power*, London: Profile Books, 2019, p. 521.

13 Michel Foucault, *The Order of Things: An Archaeology of the Human Sciences*, New York: Vintage, 1970, p. 387.

The Crisis of Truth

1 Friedrich Nietzsche, *Unpublished Writings from the Period of Unfashionable Observations*, Stanford: Stanford University Press, 1995, pp. 72f.

2 Harry G. Frankfurt, *On Bullshit*, Princeton: Princeton University Press, 2005, pp. 63f.

3 Arendt, 'Truth and Politics', p. 238.

4 Trans. note: The quoted remark is from a passage of Colbert's comedy routine at the 2006 White House Correspondents' Dinner: 'I'm sorry, I've never been a fan of books. I don't trust them. They're all fact, no heart. I mean, they're elitist, telling us what is or isn't true or what did or didn't happen. Who's Britannica to tell me the Panama Canal was built in 1914? If I want to say it was built in 1941, that's my right as an American!', at https://www.liveabout.com/stephen-colbert-white-house -correspondents-dinner-2734728.

5 Arendt, *The Origins of Totalitarianism*, p. 439. The passage following 'enormous' is omitted in the English edition. For the original German, see Hannah Arendt, *Elemente und Ursprünge totalitärer Herrschaft*, Munich: Piper, 2006, pp. 909f.

6 Adolf Hitler, *Mein Kampf: Complete and Unabridged – Fully Annotated*, New York: Reynal & Hitchcock, 1941, p. 389.

7 Ibid., p. 149.

8 Ibid., p. 234.

9 Ibid., p. 149.

10 Ibid., p. 313.

11 George Orwell, *Nineteen-Eighty-Four*, p. 44, at https:// www.planetebook.com/free-ebooks/1984.pdf.

12 Ibid., p. 6.

13 Ibid., p. 7.

14 Ibid., pp. 60f.

15 Ibid., p. 6.

16 Arendt, 'Truth and Politics', pp. 258f. (transl. amended). The German and English texts deviate. For the German, see Hannah Arendt, 'Wahrheit und Politik', in *Zwischen Vergangenheit und Zukunft: Übungen im politischen Denken I*, Munich: Piper, 2000, pp. 327–70; here: p. 363.

17 Roland Barthes, *Camera Lucida: Reflections on Photography*, London: Vintage, 2000, p. 79.

18 Luhmann, 'Entscheidungen in der "Informationsgesellschaft"'.

19 Ibid.

20 Habermas, 'Wahrheitstheorien', in *Vorstudien und Ergänzungen zur Theorie des kommunikativen Handelns*, pp. 127–82: here: p. 137.

21 Ibid., p. 136.

22 Michel Foucault, *The Government of Self and Others: Lectures at the Collège de France 1982–1983*, Basingstoke: Palgrave, 2010, p. 158.

23 Ibid., p. 157.

24 Ibid., p. 155.

25 Ibid., p. 158.

26 Michel Foucault, *The Courage of Truth: The Government of Self and Others II, Lectures at the Collège de France 1983–1984*, Basingstoke: Palgrave, 2011, p. 36. The first two passages are omitted in the English translation of Foucault's lectures.

27 Ibid., p. 79.

28 Michel Foucault, 'Die Welt ist eine große Anstalt', in

Schriften in vier Bänden: Dits et écrits, Band II: 1970–1975, Frankfurt am Main: Suhrkamp, 2002, pp. 539–40; here: p. 540; 'Le monde est un grand asile', *Dits et écrits, vol. II: 1970–1975*, Paris: Gallimard, 1994, pp. 433–4; here: p. 434.

29 Ibid.
30 Plato, *Republic* (517a), in Plato, *Complete Works*, Indianapolis: Hackett, 1997, pp. 971–1223; here: p. 1134.
31 Arendt, 'Truth and Politics', p. 264.